HERMAN
THE THIRD TREASURY

Other Popular Herman Books

The 1st Treasury of Herman
The Second Herman Treasury
Herman: The Fourth Treasury
Herman Treasury 5
Herman: The Sixth Treasury
"Herman, You Were a Much Stronger Man on Our
    First Honeymoon"
The Latest Herman
"Herman, Dinner's Served . . . as Soon as the Smoke
    Clears!"
"Herman, You Can Get in the Bathroom Now"
"They're Gonna Settle Out of Court, Herman"

HERMAN
THE THIRD TREASURY

by Jim *[signature]*

Andrews and McMeel
A Universal Press Syndicate Company
Kansas City • New York

ISBN: 0-8362-1989-9 (paperback)
       0-8362-1985-6 (cloth)
Library of Congress Catalog Card Number: 82-72416

HERMAN is syndicated internationally by Universal Press Syndicate.

First printing, August 1982
Fifteenth printing, December 1989

"**T**o me, life is like an orchard. You pick the fruit when you see it. For years, I bummed around the world looking for happiness. Then one day I realized happiness isn't something you find. All the happiness in the world is between your own two ears."

— JIM UNGER

"If you don't think you can make it into work tomorrow, give me a call."

"My ball went in the hole! What shall
I do now?"

"Make sure this one doesn't leave before
he pays his bill."

"I think I prefer the blue."

"Have you been waiting long?"

"These TV commercials are getting ridiculous!"

"I don't know whether to try to weed the lawn or tell everyone it's a vegetable garden."

"I wouldn't pay $4 admission to look at you!"

"I think we'll stay away from the jumbo-burger!"

"He'll never find the cigars, will he, Dad?"

"We don't usually accept first-grade students until they're five years old."

"Have you been at my sherry again, Wilkins?"

"Dad's gonna change the baby. I hope he gets a dog!"

"My mistake. I'm supposed to rub it on your chest."

"I think you've overwatered it!"

"You can't miss, Georgy."

"Can you send a tow truck? I'm about 300 yards inside the Lion Safari Park."

"I'd say it's your gallbladder, but if you insist on a second opinion, I'll say kidneys."

"Have you seen the latest electric model?"

"Even I can paint better than that!"

"SIT!"

"I had the spaghetti yesterday and my stomach's still working on it!"

"You won't be losing a daughter. We're going to live here!"

"Do you want the book of instructions?"

"They ALWAYS go on the warpath when we're eating!"

"Are they the new shoes you bought for $10?"

"He never said that! I saw your lips move."

"Have you given any thought to my pay raise?"

"Don't bother undressing. I'll turn up the power."

"I came in third!"

"I want you to take a half-hour walk, every day, 10 minutes before lunch."

"This may be out of your price range. It's $2."

"D'you want a dessert or coffee?"

21

"I see on your application that you used to be a termite inspector."

"I told you it was a dog movie!"

"Wanna buy a toothbrush?"

"Is that the dress you wore on our honeymoon?"

"Dad, do I get my allowance or not?"

"Can we have our horseshoe back?"

"Which one of you is General Smith?"

"My bus leaves in two minutes and I intend to be on it."

"How come you don't go fishing anymore?"

"We haven't seen a duck for two hours!"

"Got any books with nice, big, colored pictures in them, suitable for framing?"

"I'm gonna use this ball. I keep losing the other ones."

24

"I was lucky I hit the pin!"

"Not Walter . . . WATER!"

"It was a great party, Ralph."

"I think we'll get out of here before the cowboy movie starts."

"I can't figure it. These carrot plants are getting smaller!"

"I made you a nice fruitcake, but the guard said it could be used as an offensive weapon."

"I can't stand the sight of blood."

"I don't know what this is, but it's new and improved, so it must be good!"

"This stew is ruined. You said you'd be home last year!"

"I'm still not getting any hot water!"

"'Buttercup' recognized your car coming and ran off."

"I keep the door locked. I can't understand how they all got in there!"

"Stop him! He's got your dinner."

"My husband kept telling me to drive faster, Officer."

"Back to the drawing board, smarty-pants!"

"I'd let you talk more, but you're not as interesting as me."

"We need a bicycle built for two —
and one for me."

"Do you take trade-ins?"

"Don't try to tell me my job!
That's No. 37!"

"Be fair! He did ask you twice to
take it off."

"This is not the bank!"

"Have the hamburger on the house. You're the first customer who ever came back!"

"Let's hope we never have to use it!"

"When I told him it would be nice to have my breakfast in bed once in a while, he told me to sleep in the kitchen."

"Your wife's been away for three weeks now. Have you had anything to eat?"

33

"Why don't you listen? I said bring me a WENCH."

"Testing . . . testing."

"Stay there. I got the wrong one."

"Is hernia catching, Herm?"

"Members of the jury, I must ask you to disregard my last remark."

"If you want the inside cleaned, just leave your windows down."

"I've got to ask the boss for a raise tomorrow. How does this look?"

"I don't want to be a 'lookout' ANYMORE."

"Do you want to drive now?"

"Your wife's still standing in the doorway."

"Where did you get these eggs?"

"Operator, how do I make a long-distance call from here?"

"Of course it's empty! I had to hide everything."

"There's a F-I-L-E in the C-A-K-E."

"Looking at you, I'd guess your wife doesn't have exceptionally good taste!"

"Have you got a medium-sized hummingbird?"

"When I said you could have your friends
over for lunch, I meant humans."

"I want you to know I'm a firm supporter
of the ERA."

"I don't think all that natural food is doing
you any good!"

"The car wash never gets it clean."

"I said, 'Round up a POSSE'!"

"You must be hearing things: my phone wasn't ringing."

"Ho, ho, ho."

"I have to be in bed at eight, so get there about five minutes past."

"He's been filling it with food for 47 years!"

"She was doing her TV exercises and has been stuck there through three soap operas!"

"Six boxes of cookies for you, and no arguments."

"Excuse me. The machine is making a funny noise and the little light is going in a straight line."

"Here's your watch, Johnson. You're retiring early."

"Smoking or non-smoking?"

"I need as much fire insurance as I can get by next Friday night."

"That's what it says: 'one tablespoonful, 300 times a day.'"

"That guy who's filling in for you at the office is a real worker."

"I was practicing my karate and she hit me with half a brick."

"See what happens when you find them not guilty?"

"What do you want for your birthday, a battery-tester or a set of screwdrivers?"

"You heard me! Take your hat off."

"Joe's my bodyguard till I tell you where I've been all night."

"What are you asking me for?"

"This is 'Earth.' We don't hang around here too long — they're all bananas."

"Tell Sandra, lover-boy is here."

"I put two eggs in this cake."

"Twenty bucks a week on makeup and he's the best you can come up with?"

"There are more than eight cornflakes in there!"

"The doctor won't be long. Are you sure you wouldn't like a cup of coffee?"

"Going anywhere near the tropics?"

"How far can I send this cat for 30 dollars?"

"I gave your sandwich to the wrong customer. Do you still want it?"

"Why don't you have a good scream and get it over with."

"Your head's rejecting your hair transplant!"

"How many times have I told you not to start moving till I get my glasses on?"

"You were sleepwalking again last night."

"You'll have to move your lunchbox. It's blocking the fire exit."

"I think you're probably in a rut."

"I never did like dogs!"

"He's chewed through the TV cord again!"

"Your wife tells me you're making some bookshelves."

"You'll have to sit up!"

"You'd better let the cat in before he wakes up the street."

"I never said a word. He said it!"

"I finally got a day off!"

"If you ever eat turkey, you're a cannibal!"

"You'll have to wait for your soup. I can't do everything!"

"This won't take long, will it? The first race starts in 20 minutes."

"I've studied your case and I think your best bet is a tunnel!"

"You said it was getting tired. It's gone to bed!"

"Don't keep whistling."

"Don't look at me like that. It's 'evolution.'"

"I changed the baby. Now what?"

"If I bought your burglar alarm for $30, it would be the only thing in here worth stealing."

"He hates it when someone uses his bowl."

"I can't understand a word he says! Try him in Spanish."

"One step closer and I'll soak you to the skin."

"What's the big idea telling my wife you're getting a new dishwasher?"

"Don't be a spoilsport! Guess who it is."

"Keep an eye on that one."

"Can't you keep still?"

"This is one I did on my trip to Australia."

"He's half parrot and half homing pigeon.
I've sold him ten times!"

"I told you that was HIS chair!"

"What's my whisk doing in here?"

"Got one of these?"

"I thought you were gonna clean up
this kitchen."

"What are you doing?"

"Those two seem to be
enjoying themselves."

"Good luck!"

"Did you say that guy next door joined the Army?"

"I hope you haven't got gravy all over your shoes."

"Your teeth have gone in my jello!"

"Let me know if you ever need a good defense lawyer."

"Harry, the Earth isn't the third planet from the sun, is it?"

"He's got my tuna fish sandwiches again!"

"One of these hot dogs fell on the floor. You'll have to toss a coin!"

"I'll cook you a nice three-course meal during the next commercial."

"Strange how all six of your previous employers left the 'C' out of the word 'excellent.'"

"Close that door!"

"That one's genuine crocodile!"

"It's not egg on toast. It's egg OR toast!"

"D'you think we really need a kitchen?"

"Now, which pile was washed in 'Sudsy-Wudsy'?"

"You seem to have the qualifications we're looking for in a bookkeeper."

"Where's that dumb cat?"

"You can't expect me to learn the job in five minutes, can you?"

"We've got 60 guests and only three pieces of cake!"

"They shouldn't be showing girls in bikinis when kids his age are watching!"

"If you don't want to be my caddy, there are plenty of other people who do!"

"This one turns men into putty!"

"Did you tell the dog he couldn't go out tonight?"

"If he's your brother, sir, I'm sure I would have remembered him."

"Now don't mention coming in here when we get home."

"Can I borrow that magazine you were reading in bed last night?"

"How d'you expect me to plead 'guilty' or 'not guilty' when I haven't heard the evidence?"

"What's the matter with you? I'm looking for my checkbook!"

"Two months to select my jury and they found me guilty in 17 seconds."

"As it was a false alarm, I'll just give you one quick squirt."

"I want a book on speed-reading and 85 Westerns."

"I see you giving me a $20 tip!"

"Please don't slurp that soup whilst I'm trying to watch the movie."

"Gee, I thought everyone knew that
'Aquarius' and 'Leo' went well together!"

"Oh no! I've broken my nail."

"He must have heard a noise downstairs!"

"Shall I back up?"

"My hook's stuck!"

"Millions of years of evolution, and that's the latest model!"

"You'll have to come back later. They're not biting!"

"Are you 'open'?"

"It must have been that time your brother brought his portable over!"

"That was either Superman or dad falling off the roof."

"Dear Diary, the old skinflint forgot my allowance again."

"Keep it to yourself, but I've finished spending that $5 you gave me for Christmas."

"Oh dear! Look where I left poor old dad's guitar."

"We're having trouble finding 12 ex-embezzlers for the jury."

"The sink was clogged!"

"Did you fix my sewing machine?"

"Can't you work faster? My arms are killing me."

"Come on! You must admit he's 'pushy' for six months old."

"Where d'you think you're going?"

"His wife never lets him watch this show!"

"What shall we call it: ox-tail, vegetable or soup-of-the-day?"

"Watch daddy."

"I can smell cigarette smoke!"

"According to my figures, I'm 357 and you're 358."

"Mommy had this kitchen custom built."

"Can the guy downstairs borrow some milk?"

"I told you on the phone we'd be taking my new boat out."

"The old brakes failed!"

"I climbed it because it was here."

"I'll give you something to ease the pain."

"Soup or juice?"

"Not a lot of clues, Chief! We found one footprint."

"Are you sure your kid didn't mind giving up his room?"

"We specifically requested a room with a balcony!"

"I don't think 'no fixed address' is a good idea on a loan application."

"Nurse, let me know when a bell-ringer gets here."

"This is the best security device we have! Put a pair of these just inside your front door."

"You've put on weight since you quit smoking!"

MATERNITY WARD

"Anyone around?"

"He gets uncomfortable with strangers."

"He wants this book on witchcraft."

84

"Cover your left eye, madame."

"Don't talk to me during visiting hours. My wife thinks I'm in a coma."

"I can never understand your doctor's handwriting! What are your symptoms?"

"Been waiting long?"

"Do I need a return address on this?"

"Call the doctor!"

"He's having a tough time finding someone who hasn't mugged him!"

"I need 400 of these and a pair of hinges."

"Oh darling! Your very first patient."

"He's stopped playing."

"Got any books for about a dollar on financial planning?"

"Sweetheart, this will be your father-in-law."

"Whaddyer want for lunch?"

"Aren't you pleased? I made you enough sandwiches for a whole year."

"What we have here, Williams, is a breakdown in communication."

"Any requests?"

"Why can't you use your imagination and stick a few peas on there?"

"I said I was sorry!"

"The groom's late!"

"Be honest! He looks rough for 56 years old."

"No sense buying a good set 'til I know if I can play."

92

"It's called 'How to Survive on a Widow's Pension.'"

"Therefore, I leave everything to my trusted lawyer."

"If I give you a pay raise, you'll have to start worrying about tax shelters."

"Haven't you got that cork out yet?"

"I thought you were finished!"

"We were advertising for a 'driver.'"

"You're to blame for this! You let him watch 'Love Boat.'"

"You're not getting another engagement ring until you've finished paying for the other two."

"We'll do a series of x-rays starting with your wallet."

"I've got a fantastic new joke, but it's going to cost you extra."

"I'm not worried about her eloping! I'm worried about my new ladder taking the weight."

"These are expensive, but they're guaranteed up to 140 words per minute."

"If you've got any money, grab yourself a chair."

"What did you buy that for? You can't even ride a bicycle!"

"Dad, if you don't feel any better d'you want me to try acupuncture?"

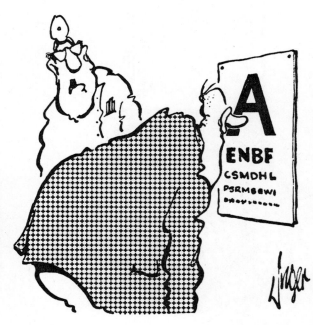

"Okay, okay, don't worry about it!"

"Watch out! One of your peas is moving."

"Who left the stereo switched on?"

"Your pulse is very, very weak!"

"Whaddyer mean, —'put him outside'? I can't even move."

"Order anything you want. I brought $4 with me."

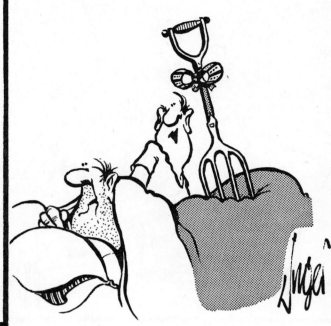

"Happy Birthday, Dad."

"Have you finished with the financial section?"

"She said she was on a diet and wiped out the salad bar."

"The invitation said 'informal dress,'
so I borrowed one from my sister."

"Watch this! This is where she hits her husband over the head with a saucepan."

"I don't like the pin placement."

"Do you feel well enough to cook?"

"You dropped your sheet of glass back there!"

"If you're gonna teach him water comes from hydrogen and oxygen, I also want him to know he can get it from a regular river."

"Dad, I need 200 'big-ones.' No questions asked."

"Your chest x-ray is fine, but your driver's license has expired."

"With my luck lately, I'd say your chances are about 50-50."

"No, it's not easy putting nine adopted kids through college on 80 smackers a week!"

"You heard me! Did I say 'rice' or 'dice'?"

"Can I borrow some of your after-shave?"

"Can you fix them by Saturday? I'm in the finals."

"You're the first guy who's moved onto this street with a bench saw!"

"Okay, that does it! No more doubles."

"Your wife told me you sold the pet crocodile."

"Is it my fault if the foreman at my last place started a fight?"

"Mom's in the penguin enclosure at the zoo, waiting for a tow truck."

"He needs a set by Friday."

"This one was painted during the French Revolution."

"I dreamt I was driving down a mountain road and the brakes failed."

105

"One Caesar's salad, no dressing."

"Don't bother getting me a baby sitter, I'm going out myself."

"D'you mind not blowing that cigarette smoke all over me."

"That's fantastic! I can't keep up with all this modern technology."

"Members of the jury, have you reached a verdict on this crook?"

"I don't know what it is! I just started here myself."

"It's funny, but I can never get any vegetables to grow along that fence!"

"Let's start again from where I said, 'Sit down!'"

"Perfect! Six feet two inches and 195 lbs."

"I'm your new neighbor, upstairs."

"We flew over one of your cities on the way in . . . very impressive!"

"I'm gonna flop here; my feet are killing me."

"As long as the waist fits, I can always fix the shoulders."

"If we split up, I want this toaster."

"They're running short of arrows!"

"It says here a laboratory rat got himself a lawyer and is suing the government for $10 million."

"See, I told you Daddy only had a 'concussion.'"

112

"D'you feel okay? That chicken was a funny color when I cooked it."

"Let me explain why I can't give you a pay raise."

'Being on a diet does not give you the right to go beserk in a donut shop."

"Why can't you watch 'The Muppets' after I've seen the news?"

"It's just for a few days, Wilkins, until her ladyship gets used to not having the old dog around."

"Shall I throw out another bag of sand?"

"What's it gonna be — an ice cream or a university education?"

"We're having a special on tonsils this week."

"I'm fixing up the room. Her mother's coming to stay with us for a week."

"Guess what happened to those sausages on the way home from the supermarket."

"Who ordered the five-star chili?"

"I know you don't like messing around with a lot of little buttons."

"My usual fee is $20 but I'll only charge
you $10."

"Cheeseburger?"

"I made us a license plate!"

"My friend, that simple piece of wire is
going to revolutionize the
garment industry!"

"I'm sorry, sir. No dogs allowed in the hotel."

"If you'd told me you had all those books, I would have made it stronger!"

"Look at his eyes! They're almost human."

"I never said you could use my boat!"

"Why didn't you say you didn't
want gravy?"

"There's nothing in the rule book that says
I can't stay here."

"Okay, slam the door as soon as
I get upstairs."

"Here grab this. I didn't have enough
money for two Strawberry Delights!"

"I said, hamburger with *fries*."

"Here it is, 'Zebra Virus'!"

"What about you! Did you see what happened?"

"This is 'Moon Over the Ocean,' painted basically from memory!"

"Do you like the new tiles I put up in the bathroom?"

"Don't overfeed the fish, nag, nag, nag."

"Have you got a room with bars on the windows?"

"If you buy a goldfish, I'll throw in the aardvark."

"I thought I told you yesterday — you can't come in without wearing a tie."

"I've been down here before! Watch out for the little guy in the fur coat."

"I wish you wouldn't talk to me when I'm nailing."

"I think you're after me!"

"My silly old key wouldn't open the front door, snuggles."

"Have a good vacation, Wilson?"

"I don't care where you're from,
I'm trying to read!"

"I'll be out of here in
30 seconds, sweetheart."

"Be careful how you sit in the chair.
It's broken."

"Keep your left arm straight and remember to follow through."

"Did you thank Grandpa for the tool kit?"

"Run upstairs and see who it is!"

"Can you fix a flat?"

"How would you like to make a few extra bucks whilst you're under the anesthetic?"

"Dad, watch me juggle!"

"My, my, he looks like his daddy!"

"Isn't he the guy you wouldn't let in last week without a tie?"

"I'm sorry — I don't have any cream."

"I know why you never write! You're too busy digging that stupid tunnel."

"Have you seen a woman on a green bike?"

"Beam me up, Scotty. It's really dead around here."

"They didn't have computer dating when we were young."

"Downstairs . . . eight letters . . . starts with 'B.'"

"Drat!"

"Is my portable TV in there again?"

"We could have flipped through your family album and saved six bucks."

"I remember the good old days when I could see the window!"

"You always lend me these old things! Why don't you splurge on an electric trimmer?"

"I told you not to bring those sandwiches in here!"

"I wonder what she sees in him!"

"Whaddyer want, 46 essential vitamins or Luke Skywalker?"

"I need a tropical fish, 18 inches by 9½ inches."

"Oh, oh! It says, 'Must be eaten before Feb. 1978.'"

"I'll have a table for you in two minutes."

"Will you get your cat off of this bed!"

"Move your foot. I think you're standing on a fried egg!"

"I thought it was you, your Majesty. I don't often forget a face."

"Do they have things like that on your planet?"

134

"Who's been using my 'Lavender Beads'?"   "I told you not to try touching your toes!"

"I hope you won't be like that on Saturday.
My sister is coming."   "Smile, Dad! We need it for school."

"It's okay, Ralph. We don't want to see your gallbladder!"

"I don't have a suitcase!"

"That's the last time I go on vacation."

"I thought this place closed at six!"

"There is another Savoy Grille downtown. Maybe you were supposed to meet her there."

"I live across the hall. Got any spare outlets you're not using?"

"You look like the Ayatollah Khomeini."

"I'm not interested in what you like. I'm the one who has to look at it."

"One of you two will be my next sales manager."

"Fired already! You were only there five weeks."

"I'm sorry, sir, you'll have to return to your seat. We'll be landing in a few minutes."

"Don't forget, Grandpa — when my friends get here, I told them you knew Julius Caesar."

"I don't suppose you remembered to put up my picture!"

"Is it OK if I scream with agony between answering the questions?"

"Joycey, what's the best stuff for split ends?"

"I don't care *who* she votes for. I'm not kissing a kid with measles!"

"Do we have any more boxes of 'Fruity-Scoops'?"

"I just got fired, so I'll wait for my tip outside the front door!"

"Open the door. It's only Mother."

"Can I exchange this for 'Doggo-Chunks'?"

"They look a lot bigger on TV!"

"He tied a knot."

"Is that for a pool?"

"Guess what! I sold that piece of pork pie."

"I can watch as much crime and violence as I like as long as they all keep their clothes on."

"He's known about us for years. They've locked him up twice!"

"What do you want, Warden? I'm really busy!"

"He said this stuff made his hair turn purple."

"Ring it again."

144

"I can't even pronounce what you've got!"

"Grab your shepherd's pie. It's fourth from the top."

"If you spend over $20, it includes free vehicle insurance against vandalism in our parking lot."

"Go and find the nearest town and plug this in."

"Breaker-one-nine, breaker-one-nine. I need a glass of water."

"At least try the earrings! This lot cost me $6."

"Gold's gone up to 87 cents an ounce!"

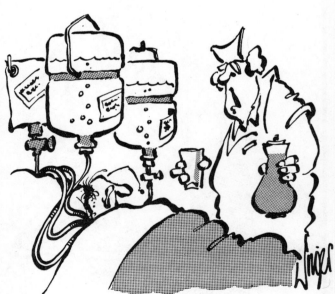

"You're not drinking your water!"

"That lifeguard said, 'Tell your wife to stay out of the shipping lanes.'"

"What does that mean, 'Merchandise returned at your own risk'?"

"He said he wanted the menu back to have a good laugh."

"I think I just found your other blue sock."

"Watch out for that big fella when you wash the insides."

"Aren't you dressed yet! My mother will be here in five minutes."

"This is a double celebration! I've been open six months and you're my sixth customer."

"I have two daughters! Why do you insist on White Fawn and not Galloping Buffalo?"

"Take two of these with meals but no more than 30 a day."

"Hand over all the cash or
he starts playing."

"My pottery teacher says it shows
great promise."

"Albert hasn't worked here for 15 years."

"I'm not going to ask him.
You ask him."

"He ate that whole chocolate cake in the 'fridge to protest the current economic situation in Poland."

"There's someone here now, Steve. I'll call you back in five minutes."

"What is it this time?"

"You lump! I said write, 'Happy Birthday, Ralph' on *that* one."

"Is that the one who forgot his wedding anniversary?"

"D'you wanna wait for the next one?"

"Don't play with Dad's pulley!"

"He's swallowed my clockwork mouse!"

"How about a bottle of aftershave
for her legs?"

"D'you wanna buy any
Girl Scout cookies?"

"Every one of the ten character references
you provided said you owed them money."

"I don't need the warranty. I'll bring it back
if it doesn't work."

"If you're going out, don't let us stop you." "Did you hear me whining when your show was on?"

"We're having a tough time managing on your son's allowance." "See what happens when you have too many walkies!"

"Hold on! Back up to that part about 'love, honor and obey.'"

"Stand by for the earthquake."

"I hired you to sweep the floor. Leave the customers alone!"

"'Harry,' she said, 'I wanna marry you for your money!' And we've been happy ever since."

"Where were you?"

"Charlie Innertube, one day your name will be a household word!"

"He was trapped on a ledge, 36 floors up."

"I like the facelift, but my wife thinks my ears are a touch too high."

"That's nice! You show up and all the
gorillas run inside."

"D'you mind not shouting 'peanuts' while this court is in session?"

"D'you want a really good tip?"

"How come he's got a leg *and* a wing?"

161

"I think he's even taller than I was at his age."

"Now I need enough paint for two mountains, five trees and a small lake."

"If we sue for half a million, there should be a couple of hundred in it for you."

"Oh no! That was going straight in the treble-20."

"You said you wanted a large family."

"Which credit card d'you want — R.G. Williams, Miss S. Peters or the Rev. J. Thomas?"

"It's homemade alphabet soup!"

"It says 'Do not feed.' Look at your best coat!"

163

"Dad, which part of the chicken is the noodle?"

"Have you got any books on how to overcome shyness?"

"That bamboo chair you sold me is still alive!"

"I think for our own safety, we should leave this lot alone for another few thousand years."

"Sorry about the inconvenience! We're having the ceiling painted."

"That's a good speech! It's the way you're reading it."

"I could have been Miss Universe, but they didn't have space travel in those days."

"Oh, please! I promise I won't mess it up like last time."

"Go and tell Mommy that Daddy forgot his key."

"I've nearly finished this. Got any furniture polish?"

"Why don't you pick on someone your own size?"

"They're almost human!"

"Something tells me I'm in for a very long day."

"If she's a genetic reject, how come I have to chase off all the young guys around here with a stick?"

"An eagle came straight through the ceiling and grabbed the goldfish."

"When are they supposed to be coming to fix that T.V.?"

"Are you sure you're comfortable like that!"

"Is that you? You've only been surfing five minutes!"

"I didn't have a button, so I cut the hole off."

"I'll have to charge extra for that one."

"You told me on the phone that you were a six-footer!"

"He's swallowed $4 in small change! Can you operate before the stores close?"

"That was close! We won by two votes."

"The good news is, I've saved you five bucks at the car wash tomorrow."

"Okay, my good woman. We'll go with the ole strawberry shortcake and four spoons."

"D'you want your coffee now, captain?
We've hit an iceberg."

"Maybe we're over-drawn!"

"Don't stop singing! You've got
a nice voice."

"It comes with three vegetables: two peas
and a carrot."

"Did he say he was coming back, or what?"

"I made two dozen chocolate chip cookies. Can you eat all of them?"

"I'd say I pretty much run things around here."

"You just poured boiling oil over the window cleaner!"

"Tell Williams I've decided to make him the new manager in Hawaii."

"You want it to look lifelike, don't you?"

"Wait there while I tie up the dog."

"Can I sit up in the front of the plane?"

175

"Grandma, if you bought a motorbike, we could both use it!"

"As my official food-taster, you'll be upholding the proud tradition of your 16 predecessors."

"I reviewed your salary, as you requested. We're paying you too much!"

"I'm not going to tell you again, buddy; get out of those flowers."

"Do you feel anything yet?"

"It went around twice and stopped on 18."

"Tell me a funny joke. He'll stop you if I've heard it."

"Who ordered the giant clams?"

"I'll get the check. Pass your money under the table."

"I can only see two in there! Did one escape?"

"Yes, skydiving! He's going for his first jump tomorrow."

"I don't care who you are! Take your hat off in this restaurant."

"That jogging certainly seems to be getting your weight down."

"D'you want the piano in the living room?"

"There's a monk trapped in the elevator."

"It's not my fault we haven't got your size!
Try Camping Equipment on the third floor."

"Tell him! I was here first, wasn't I?"

181

"I'm warning you, Rodney, I want you home by ten o'clock and no later."

"You're a real prize, you are, Bentley!"

"I've only got two pairs of hands you know!"

"I wish you wouldn't buy this cheap catsup."

"This is my wife's twin brother Arnold."

"Every cloud has a silver lining! Now you've got two swords."

"Can the police give you a speeding ticket in a car wash?"

"Have you got this same chair in dark brown?"

"I got the car in the garage, but I had to go through the kitchen."

"Your brother got a job in a wallpaper factory."

"I don't usually borrow stuff from strangers, but I like your face."

"Why do they call you 'the elephant man'? You look perfectly normal to me."

"You gotta be real fast when you're painting ducks!"

"I let my sister use the hammock."

"Quick, take a look! There's a guy walking out of our house carrying the T.V."

"Too big?"

"All I can say is, I'm glad I didn't eat any of it!"

"This is called 'Reclining Nude.' I don't think the children should be looking at it."

"I thought so! You're not chewing your food."

"Does that say 'help wanted'?"

"I know we haven't got your size without even looking!"

"Anything for 22A?"

"Biggest bug I ever saw!"

"You've been overfeeding my horse again, Smithers?"

"When you grow up, make sure you marry a mechanic."

"Can I buy half of one and get the other half free?"

"Listen, kid — if I sold you a pair of roller skates, I'd lay awake nights worrying."

"Here, you wanted to be plant manager. Take care of this!"

"I'm looking for an uninhabited island with fantastic night life."

"Maybe it's some sort of omen!"

"Did you fire Williams in
'Fruit & Vegetables'?"

"I can't get comfortable!"

"He only went hunting once."

"D'you wanna stay here tonight or sleep on the beach and eat?"

"Cleo, get off of there and let this nice man sit down."

"Can you get that guy's teeth out of there?"

"You look just as bad as you did when you went in!"

"I'll have a teeny-bopper-burger-razzle and she wants a coffee."

"My wife bought this and I want to return it."

"I wish you'd sit down, Lily. I never win when you keep pacing around."

"I make mistakes to keep you on your toes!"

"Whatever made you think plant food would make your hair grow?"

"Don't look at me! Look to the front."

"It's either two guys carrying a canoe or a long horse wearing sneakers."

"I want to report a missing husband."

"Is that your idea of exercise — buying a book on jogging?"

"Look what your dog did to my costume!"

"Lily, give me a price on those bee-keeper hats."

"Someone broke in while we were asleep. They left $10!"

"We'll have to have dinner out; the toaster's broken."

"Nice shot! That one crossed 12 lanes and wiped out the cigarette machine."

"How did things go down at the old divorce court?"

"I like it fairly short and parted in the middle."

"Want me to try to get you a private ward?"

"There's the check and here's a photo of my wife and kids."

"Room 1708 doesn't have a plug for the bath!"

"If we don't find a gas station soon, Wilkins, I'm going to have to take a rest."

"As soon as I got married,
I saved every spare nickel. Now
I've got eight bucks!"

"Large coffee to go and make
sure the lid's on tight."

"If you get any worse, can I
keep your paint roller?"

"Your job application says
you like meeting the public."

"Are these green ones emeralds?"

"I see you spent the last
12 years in the Navy."

"How did you say that without
moving your lips?"

"That guy who said the coffee tasted
funny left without paying!"

"Your honor, with 85 previous
acquittals, my client has
a faultless record."

"I know what you got me for my birthday. It was on the 11 o'clock news."

"Banana milkshake and two straws."

"You're absolutely certain this one's mine?"

"Are both of you suffering from double vision?"

"*Tea*! I said I wanted a small tea!"

"Pull out as much as you want."

"I fell asleep on the beach, reading a newspaper."

"Remember, only bend the ones which are not marked 'do not bend.'"

"Either you buy me a bike or I'm gonna get myself adopted."

"Cash or charge?"

"Dad, I'm starting grade six soon. I guess this is where 'the generation gap' begins."

"It says right here. You're not supposed to open the lid during the spin cycle."

"It's marked 'urgent' so I read it
on the way over."

"It's homemade bread! D'you want
two slices?"

"I nearly didn't come with all that rain."

"Let's go, Rex. It's time for
your piano lessons."

"Come on! Tell the nice man how much you want to borrow."

"He was an unmanageable 6'2" tall when I married him."

"Nobody's leaving! Why don't you start singing one of your songs."

"Take one capsule tonight, and if there's no improvement by tomorrow morning, take the whole bottle."